FORCES
AND
MOTION

Chris Oxlade

An imprint of Hodder Children's Books

Titles in the *Science Files* series:

Electricity and Magnetism • Forces and Motion • Light and Sound • The Solar System

Science Files is a simplified and updated version of Hodder Wayland's
Science Fact Files.

**For more information on this series and other Hodder Wayland titles,
go to www.hodderwayland.co.uk**

Text copyright © Hodder Wayland 2005

Editor: Katie Sergeant
Designer: Simon Borrough
Typesetter: Victoria Webb
Illustrator: Alex Pang

First published in Great Britain in 1999 by Macdonald Young Books,
an imprint of Wayland Publishers Ltd
This edition updated and published in 2005 by Hodder Wayland,
an imprint of Hodder Children's Books

Oxlade, Chris
    Forces and motion. – (Science files)
    1.Force and energy – Juvenile literature 2.Motion
    Juvenile literature
    I.Title
    531.1

ISBN 0750247088

Printed in China by WKT Company Ltd

Hodder Children's Books
A division of Hodder Headline Limited
338 Euston Road, London NW1 3BH

Cover picture: Pendulum swinging, close-up.
Endpaper picture: At a wind farm, the energy of the wind is used to produce electricity.
Title page picture: Skydivers falling towards the Earth.

We are grateful to the following for permission to reproduce photographs:
Getty Images/Taxi cover (Ken Reid); Robert Harding Picture Library 11 (Jeremy Bright); Science Photo Library front 9 top (Prof Harold Edgerton), 9 bottom (Philippe Plailly), 13 (Richard Megna/Fundamental Photos), 14 (Michael Dalton/Fundamental Photos), 16 (NASA), 22 (Keith Kent), 24 (Peter Menzel), 27 (Dick Luria), 28 (Adam Hart-Davis), 30 (George Haling), 33 (Steve Grand), 35 (Kaj R Svensson), 36 top (NASA), 37 (Lawrence Berkeley), 40 (US Library of Congress), 41 (Stanford Linear Accelerator Center), 43 (Mehau Kulyk); Stock Market 5, 8, 10–11, 18, 19 (Tom Sanders/Photri), 31 (CH Jones), 36 bottom, 38 (Tom Ives), 39 (David Lawrence); Tony Stone Images 17 (Bob Thomason). Remaining photos are courtesy of Digital Vision.

The website addresses (URLs) included in this book were valid at the time of going to press. However, because of the nature of the Internet, it is possible that some addresses may have changed, or sites may have changed or closed down since publication. While the author and Publishers regret any inconvenience this may cause the readers, no responsibility for any such changes can be accepted by either the author or the Publisher.

Contents

Words in **bold** can be found in the glossary on page 44.

Introduction

The world is full of movement. There are people walking, running and playing, trucks and trains travelling along, birds flying, clouds moving across the sky and leaves rustling on the trees. None of these movements would happen without forces. A force is simply a push or pull that acts on an object.

Forces often change the way things are moving. A push or pull on a stationary object may make the object start to move. A push or pull on a moving object may make the object move faster or slower, stop moving, change direction, or spin round.

The force of the wind pushes on a yacht's sails, which push the yacht through the water.

A bent pole makes the force that lifts a pole vaulter over the bar.

FACT FILE

FUNDAMENTAL FORCES

Although forces are made in dozens of different ways, there are actually only five types of force. Scientists call these the 'fundamental forces'. They are: **gravity**, electrical forces, magnetic forces, and two nuclear forces, the strong nuclear force and the weak nuclear force.

Gravity is the force that attracts objects to each other. The electrical force happens between electrical charges. The magnetic force happens between moving electrical charges. The nuclear forces only happen inside the **nucleus** of an **atom**. We hardly ever see their effects.

A computer *simulation* of an atom splitting up. The split is caused by the weak nuclear force.

MORE EFFECTS OF FORCES

Forces don't always change the movement of objects. They have other effects, too. For example, pulling on the two ends of an elastic band makes the elastic band stretch, rather than move. And pushing on two sides of a ball of dough squashes it.

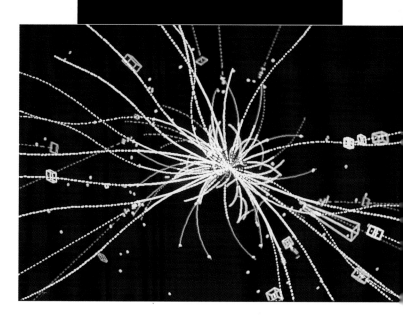

Gravity

When you hold up an object and let go of it, it falls to the ground. It is pulled downwards by the force of gravity. Gravity is the force that attracts objects to each other. Things fall because of gravity between them and the Earth.

GRAVITY FROM MASS

Gravity happens between all objects that have **mass**. Mass is the amount of **matter** in an object. It depends on how many atoms and molecules the object contains, and the chemical elements that they are made of. Mass is measured in grams and kilograms. The greater the mass of an object, the greater its pull of gravity on other objects. But the mass must be huge for us to notice its effect.

A rock climber is always fighting against gravity trying to pull him downwards.

 **FACT FILE**

JUMPING ON THE MOON

The Moon's gravity is much smaller than the Earth's gravity. So it is easier to jump into the air on the Moon than on the Earth. In fact, you can jump about six times higher. On Jupiter, gravity is much greater than on Earth, so it would be harder to jump.

HISTORY FILE

ISAAC NEWTON (1642-1727)

Isaac Newton was the first scientist to realise that the force that keeps the Moon in orbit round the Earth was the same as the force that makes objects fall to the ground. He also wrote down laws of motion that describe how objects move (see page 22).

GRAVITY AND WEIGHT

Weight is not the same thing as mass. We often see weight measured in kilograms on packets, but in science this is incorrect. Weight is actually the force of gravity between the Earth and an object. The mass of an object always stays the same, but its weight can change if it moves to a place where gravity is different.

The force of gravity between objects gets smaller as the distance between them gets bigger. So thousands of kilometres away from Earth, the weight of an object is much less than it is on the surface. Millions of kilometres out in space, far from any star or planet, objects are weightless.

Tides are caused by the gravity of the Moon and Sun, which make water slosh about in the oceans. This makes the water rise and fall along coasts.

Electric and Magnetic Forces

Electric and magnetic forces are very closely linked together. They are both caused by electric charges. Electric charges are carried by the tiny particles that make up atoms. These charges can be positive or negative.

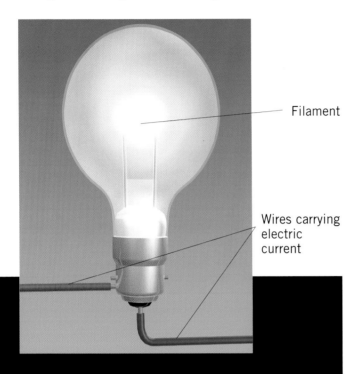

Filament

Wires carrying electric current

When a light bulb is lit, about three million million electrons pass through the bulb's filament every second.

 **FACT FILE**

ELECTRONS
An electron is a tiny particle that is part of an atom. It has a negative electric charge. An electric current in a wire is made up of a flow of electrons. These electrons are free to move from atom to atom in the wire.

THE ELECTRIC FORCE
Objects normally contain the same number of positive and negative charges, which cancel each other out. But objects can gain or lose charges, and end up with an overall negative or positive charge. For example, if you rub a balloon with a woollen cloth, the balloon becomes negatively charged and the woollen cloth becomes positively charged.

Particles or objects with the same electric charge (they are either both positive or both negative) push each other away, or repel each other. Particles or objects with opposite charges (one negative and one positive) pull towards, or attract each other. The closer the charges are to each other, the stronger the force between them is.

Two rubbed balloons side by side repel each other. A charged balloon also attracts hairs and small bits of paper. This happens because the negative charge in the balloon attracts positive charges in the hair or paper to the surface.

THE MAGNETIC FORCE
The magnetic force happens between two electric charges that are moving. In magnets the force is made by **electrons** moving around their atoms. An electric current is made up of moving charge, so two wires with currents flowing in them also attract or repel each other.

MAGNETIC FIELDS AND POLES

A permanent magnet is a piece of material that makes a magnetic force all the time. Permanent magnets are made from materials such as iron, nickel and cobalt. The space around a magnet or a current-carrying wire where its magnetic force can be felt is called a **magnetic field**.

A magnet always has two areas where its magnetic force is strongest. These are called its poles. The poles are called the north pole and south pole. Two like poles (two norths or two souths) on different magnets always repel each other, and two opposite poles (a north and a south) always attract each other.

The Earth has a magnetic field that stretches far out into space.

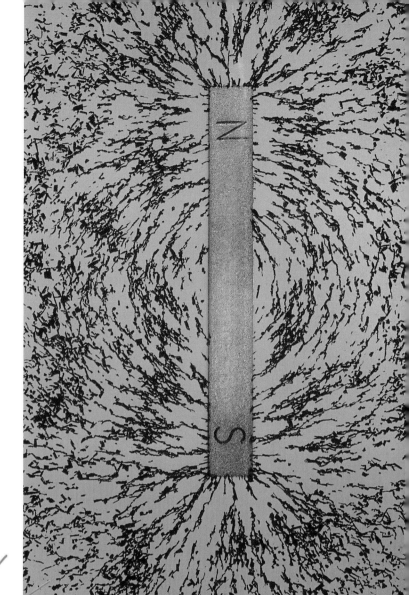

Iron filings scattered around a magnet show up the magnet's magnetic field.

North magnetic pole

Earth

Lines of magnetic force. The magnetic field is strongest where the lines are closest together.

South magnetic pole

13

Measuring Forces

Forces can be very large or very small. For example, a huge force is needed to launch a massive rocket upwards against gravity, but an insect with a very small mass needs only a very tiny force to jump into the air.

Forces are measured in units called newtons (N). The unit is named after the English scientist Isaac Newton (see page 11). One newton is the force needed to make a mass of 1 kilogram speed up by 1 metre per second. On Earth's surface, a 100 gram (0.1 kilogram) mass weighs about 1 newton.

HISTORY FILE

WEIGHING THE EARTH

In 1798, the English scientist Henry Cavendish (1731-1810) calculated the mass of the Earth. He carefully measured the force of gravity between two very heavy lead balls. This told him how strong gravity is between two known masses. He used this to calculate how heavy the Earth must be to make its pull of gravity on objects. His answer was 6,000 billion billion tonnes, almost exactly the same as modern scientists have calculated.

Measuring weight with a spring balance.

A very accurate balance is called a chemical balance. This is used to measure mass rather than force, so it is marked in grams instead of newtons.

As the block moves along the surface the spring balance shows the *friction* pulling on the block.

Block of wood

Spring balance

Smooth surface

BALANCES

We measure forces with a device called a spring balance. Inside a spring balance is a spring with a pointer on its end. The force being measured pulls on the end of the spring. The bigger the force, the more the spring stretches, moving the pointer further along the scale. The scale is marked in newtons.

Friction is greater on a rough surface.

TEST FILE

MEASURING FRICTION

You can use a spring balance to measure the force of friction. Friction is the force that tries to stop surfaces sliding against each other. It is larger when surfaces are rough and pushed together harder. Place a wooden block on a smooth surface and attach the spring balance to it. Slowly pull on the balance until the block begins to move, and write down the reading on the balance. Try the experiment again, using the same block but on a rough surface instead.

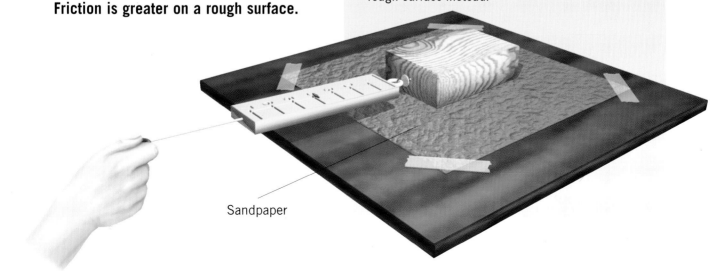

Sandpaper

Forces Working Together

The forces of *lift* and weight combine to keep an aircraft flying level.

It is rare for an object to have just one force acting on it. Most have two forces acting on them, and some have three or more.

For example, when you are sitting on a chair, you have two forces acting on you. They are

FACT FILE

VECTORS

Most quantities that we measure, such as mass, energy and time, have only size. But a force has direction as well as size. A force of 3 newtons acting in one direction is different to a force of 3 newtons acting in the opposite direction. We say that force is a **vector quantity**. **Velocity** and **acceleration**, that we see later in the book, are vector quantities, too.

your weight pulling downwards, and the chair pushing upwards.

An aeroplane has four forces acting on it. They are its weight pulling down, lift from its wings pushing up, thrust from its engines pushing forwards, and friction from the air pulling backwards.

ADDING FORCES

When two or more forces are acting on an object, we add the forces to find out the overall force that is acting. This overall force is called the **resultant force**. For example, if there are two horses pulling forwards on a cart, each with a force of 1,000 newtons, the resultant force is 2,000 newtons, also pulling forwards. It is important to say what the direction of each force is because force is a vector quantity. In this example, if the horses pulled in different directions to each other, the resultant force on the cart would be different.

Forces from three tugs add together to make the force that pulls this oil platform.

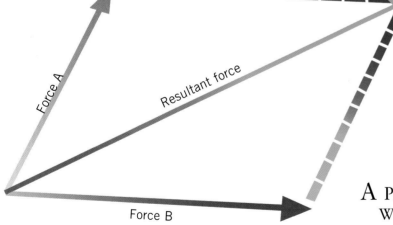

A parallelogram of forces used to find the resultant force made up by two forces (A and B) acting in different directions.

A PARALLELOGRAM OF FORCES

When two forces do not act in the same direction, it is more difficult to add them together. We have to draw a diagram called a parallelogram of forces. The direction and length of the arrows in the diagram show the direction and size of the force. The sides of the parallelogram are the two forces, and the diagonal is the resultant.

17

The weightlifter pushes the bar upwards with a force that equals its weight.

Balanced Forces

TEST FILE

FIND THE CENTRE OF MASS

Punch a small hole in the edge of a piece of card and hang the card on a paper clip. Hang a string with a weight on the end of the paper clip, too. Hold just the clip and let them swing freely. When they have stopped moving draw a line on the card in line with the string. Now punch a new hole in the card and do the same again. The card's centre of mass is where the two lines cross.

When two forces of the same size act on an object, but in opposite directions, they cancel each other out. The resultant force is zero. The forces continue to push and pull, but they balance each other. The object is said to be in **equilibrium** because the forces on it are balanced.

For example, when you are standing still, there are two forces acting on you: gravity is pulling down and the ground is pushing up. The two forces balance each other, and you are in equilibrium.

All stationary objects on the Earth are in equilibrium, otherwise they would start to move. Moving objects can be in equilibrium, too. For example, a car moving at constant velocity is in equilibrium because the force from its engine pulling forwards is balanced by friction trying to slow it down.

THE CENTRE OF GRAVITY

The centre of gravity of an object is the place where an object's mass seems to be concentrated. For example, the centre of mass of a pencil is right in the middle.

An object is in equilibrium if its centre of gravity is stationary or moving at constant velocity. It can be spinning round its centre of gravity, and still be in equilibrium.

 **FACT FILE**

TERMINAL VELOCITY

When an object is moving through the air, the air pushes on it in the opposite direction to the direction the object is travelling. This force is called **air resistance** or drag. Air resistance increases with speed. A falling object is acted upon by gravity pulling downwards and drag pushing upwards. As it begins to fall air resistance is small and it accelerates. It falls faster and faster until the air resistance becomes as large as gravity, and the forces balance. Now the object falls at a steady speed, known as **terminal velocity**.

Skydivers with their legs and arms spread reach a terminal velocity of about 200 kilometres per hour.

Speed, Velocity and Acceleration

Speed is a measure of how far an object moves in a certain amount of time. It is normally measured in metres per second or kilometres per hour. For example, if a car travelled 100 metres in five seconds, its speed would be 20 metres per second.

Average speed is the speed of an object averaged over a certain time. Imagine a train that travels between two cities 200 kilometres apart, stopping at stations in between. If it completed the journey in two hours, its average speed would 100 kilometres per hour.

TEST FILE

MEASURING AVERAGE SPEED

On a playing field, use a tape measure to mark out a track 50 metres long. Ask a friend to run from one end to the other, and time how long they take with a stopwatch. To find their average speed in metres per second, divide the distance (50 metres) by the time in seconds.

A car travelling at constant speed.

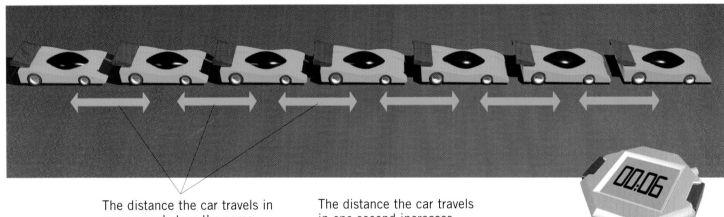

The distance the car travels in one second stays the same.

The distance the car travels in one second increases.

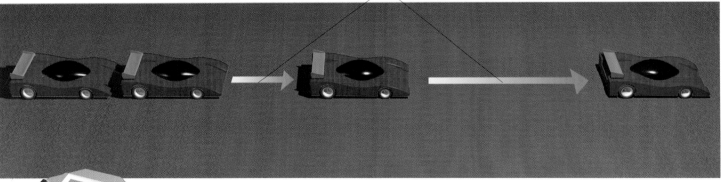

A car accelerating.

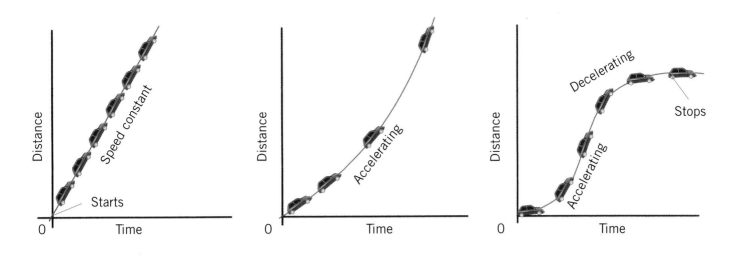

Distance | Time | Starts | Speed constant | 0

Distance | Time | Accelerating | 0

Distance | Time | Decelerating | Stops | Accelerating | Accelerating | 0

FACT FILE

DISTANCE-TIME GRAPHS

We can show the speed of an object on a distance-time graph, which shows how far an object has travelled after a certain amount of time. At steady speed the line is straight. A line getting steeper shows acceleration, and a line getting less steep shows negative acceleration, or deceleration.

VELOCITY

Velocity is sometimes confused with speed, but it is slightly different. Velocity is speed in a certain direction. It is a vector quantity so it has direction as well as size. Imagine a ball swinging round on the end of a string. Its speed stays the same, but its velocity changes because it keeps changing direction.

ACCELERATION

Acceleration is a change in velocity. It is measured by how much the velocity changes in a second. Its units are metres per second per second. Imagine that a cyclist accelerates from a velocity of 2 metres per second to a velocity of 3 metres per second in 1 second. The acceleration is 1 metre per second per second.

On Earth, the acceleration of a falling object is 9.8 metres per second per second. This is called the acceleration due to gravity.

The two balls accelerate towards the ground at exactly the same rate, and hit the ground at the same time, even though the pink ball is moving sideways.

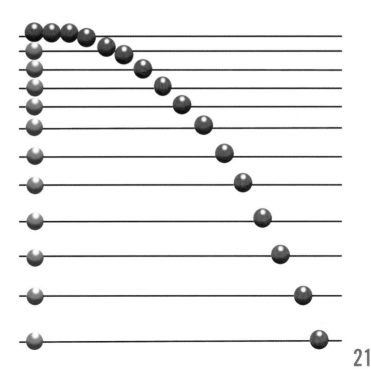

The Laws of Motion

When we say that an object is in motion, we normally mean it is moving along or spinning round. Objects don't start moving unless a force pushes or pulls them. And they carry on moving unless a force slows them down again.

The Thrust Supersonic Car being accelerated forwards by the thrust from its engines.

FACT FILE

NEWTON'S LAWS OF MOTION

Isaac Newton (see page 11) wrote down three laws of motion which describe how a force changes the motion of an object.

• Newton's first law: An object will stay still or keep moving at constant velocity unless a force acts on it.

• Newton's second law: If a force acts on an object, the object will accelerate in the direction of the force. The greater the force, the greater the acceleration.

• Newton's third law: Forces always act in pairs. If a force acts on an object, then the object exerts an equal but opposite force on the object making the original force. These forces are called action and reaction.

Ball thrown
forwards

If you stand on a skateboard and throw a heavy ball forwards, the ball pushes you backwards. This is action and reaction at work.

Skateboard rolls
backwards

Imagine a spacecraft in space far from the gravity of any planets. It keeps moving in the same direction at a constant speed because no forces act on it. There is no air resistance to slow it down, so it needs no thrust from its engines to keep it going.

INERTIA AND MOMENTUM

If you push on an object, the object seems to resist your push. This effect is called **inertia**. The greater an object's mass, the greater its inertia. That means it is harder to get moving, and harder to stop. All moving objects also have a property called **momentum**. It is an object's mass multiplied by its velocity.

TEST FILE

ACTION AND REACTION

Warning: Ask an adult to help you with this experiment. Make sure that the cork will not hit anybody when it flies from the bottle.

Put a few tablespoons of vinegar into a plastic drinks bottle. Wrap some baking powder in tissue paper, twist the ends tightly, and drop it into the bottle. Quickly push a cork into the bottle neck, lie the bottle on its side and wait. The vinegar and baking powder will react together to make gas, which will push the cork from the bottle. This force is the action. The cork pushes back on the bottle, making it move forwards. This is the reaction.

Newton's first law at work! There is no force to stop the rider's motion.

Forces, Work and Energy

orces and **work** always go together.
Scientists say that work is done when a
force moves an object. The bigger the force
and the further the object moves, the greater
the amount of work that is done. For
example, you do more work if you lift a
heavy book up to a high shelf than you do
if you lift a lighter book up to a low shelf.
Work is measured in units called joules (J).

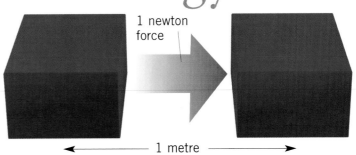

1 newton force

1 metre

One joule is the amount of work done when a force of 1 newton moves an object a distance of 1 metre.

ENERGY

Scientists say that energy is the ability to do
work. For example, you need energy to lift
a book on to a shelf. Energy is measured in
joules, too. In the world of motion, there are
two main types of energy – **kinetic energy**
and **potential energy**.

Solar-powered cars change light energy from the Sun into kinetic energy with solar cells and electric motors.

The water has both kinetic energy (because it is moving) and potential energy (because it is above the ground). Some of this energy is changed to kinetic energy in the wheel.

Water flows on to wheel

Energy of water turns wheel

Kinetic energy is the energy an object has because it is moving. The faster an object is moving and the greater its mass, the more kinetic energy it has.

Potential energy is the energy an object has because of where it is. For example, an object has more potential energy when it is on a high shelf than on a low shelf. This is because more work was done to put the object in that position.

Energy comes in many other forms, too. For example, heat, light, sound, chemical and electricity are all forms of energy. However, these are not forms of energy that are to do with the motion of objects.

CHANGING ENERGY

Energy can change from one form to another. Imagine dropping a book on to the floor. When the book is above the floor it has potential energy. As it falls, the potential energy turns to kinetic energy. When the book hits the floor, the kinetic energy turns into sound energy.

FACT FILE

COUNTING ENERGY AND WORK

- Kinetic energy of family car moving at 100 kilometres per hour = 500,000 joules.
- Work done climbing flight of stairs = 1,000 joules.
- Chemical energy in a day's food = 10,000,000 joules.

At a power station, energy in fuel is changed into electrical energy.

Conservation of Energy

One of the most important laws in science is called the law of conservation of energy. The law says that energy cannot be made, and it cannot be destroyed. It can only be changed from one form into another. Sometimes energy seems to disappear, but it never actually does. It just gets turned into forms of energy that we can't see, such as heat.

Many inventors have tried to build *perpetual motion* machines that keep working without any energy being put in. They never work because some energy is always lost because of friction.

Energy moves to and fro between the swinging pendulums.

TEST FILE

SWINGING PENDULUMS

Ask an adult to help you to stretch a string across a doorway. Hang two pendulums from the string. Use weights such as bags of coins or sand, or bunches of large metal washers. Make sure that the two strings are the same length.

Gently push one of the pendulums to make it start swinging. Gradually this pendulum will stop swinging and the second one will start swinging. Then the first one will start swinging again. Energy is being transferred between the pendulums.

Imagine throwing a bean bag straight upwards. The bag starts with plenty of kinetic energy. But after you release the bag, it gradually slows down until it stops going upwards. The kinetic energy seems to have been lost. But it hasn't. It has turned to potential energy instead. We can see this energy as the bag falls back to the ground, and the potential energy gradually turns back to kinetic energy. The kinetic energy seems to disappear when the bag hits the ground. But it is turned into sound energy that we hear as a thud, and heat energy in the bag and the surface that it lands on. If you don't count the energy that is lost through air resistance, the bean bag returns to you with the same amount of energy as it had when you threw it.

When snooker balls collide, the total kinetic energy of the balls remains the same before and after the collision.

Machines

LEVERS

A **lever** is made up of a bar that can pivot around a point, called the **fulcrum**. A lever can make the effort applied to it larger or smaller. For example, the lever below can be used to lift a heavy object using a small effort. Levers are found in scissors, pliers, tin openers and many other simple devices.

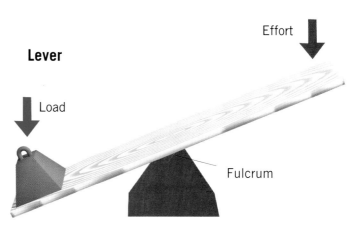

Lever

Effort

Load

Fulcrum

In science, a machine is a simple device that makes it easier to move something. The force that the machine is trying to overcome is called the **load**. The force applied to the machine is called the **effort**. In this pulley system, the load is the weight of the object and the effort is the pull on the string. The system makes the effort smaller than the load, making it easy to lift heavy objects.

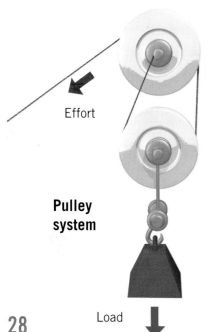

Effort

Pulley system

Load

INCLINED PLANES

An inclined plane is a simple machine made up of a slope or a ramp. The effort needed to lift an object up a slope is not as big as the effort needed to lift it straight up.

FACT FILE

POWER

Power is a measure of how quickly energy changes from one form to another. In a machine such as a car engine or oven, it is a measure of how much energy the machine gives out. The unit of power is the watt (W), equal to one joule per second.

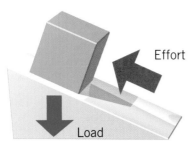

Inclined plane

Load

Effort

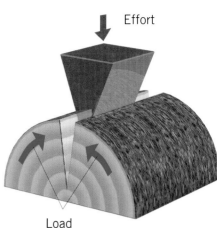

Effort

A wedge works like two inclined planes, which make it easier to push or pull things apart.

Load

WHEELS AND AXLES

A wheel and axle is a simple machine made up of a wheel attached to the end of an axle or rod. It works because the wheel is larger than the axle. The wheel makes it easier to turn the rod. A door knob and a car steering wheel are examples of wheels and axles.

Effort

Load

Wheel and axle

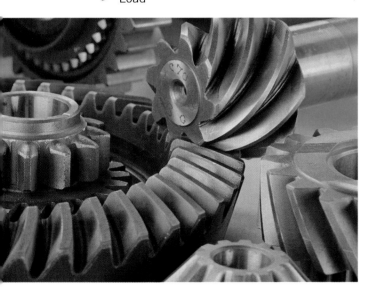

Gear wheels work on the principle of the wheel and axle.

HISTORY FILE

ARCHIMEDES

Archimedes was a scientist in ancient Greece. He lived from about 287 BC to about 212 BC. Archimedes studied how machines such as levers and pulleys worked. He was also a talented mathematician.

Archimedes invented this machine for lifting water from rivers into fields to water crops. It is now known as the Archimedean screw.

Turning Forces

Forces can make objects turn round instead of start moving, speed up, or slow down. For example, when you push on the side of a playground roundabout, the roundabout turns round. To make an object turn, you have to make a push or pull that is not lined up with the object's centre of mass or the place where it is pivoted.

A spanner makes a large turning force on a nut or bolt.

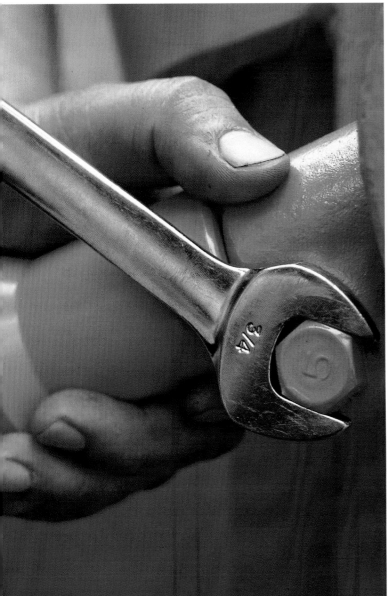

 **TEST FILE**

A BALANCED SEE-SAW
Make a model see-saw with a pencil and a ruler. Put the ruler across the pencil so that it is in balance and can tip from side to side. Put a coin on each end of the ruler and try to balance it again. Now add another coin to one end and try to balance it again. You'll have to move the two coins closer to the pencil. Can you see that a coin further from the fulcrum turns the ruler more?

This object has a weight in the base. It always returns to a position of equilibrium.

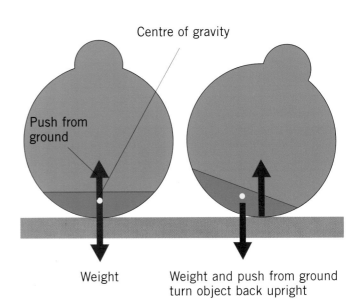

Centre of gravity

Push from ground

Weight

Weight and push from ground turn object back upright

MOMENTS

The **turning effect** of a force is called its **moment**. The further from the centre of gravity or from a pivot the line of a force is, the greater the moment. That's why it's easier to turn a nut with a long spanner than with a short spanner.

EQUILIBRIUM

Turning forces on an object often cancel each other out. When this happens, the object is said to be in equilibrium. For example, if two people with equal weights sit on opposite ends of a see-saw, the see-saw balances, so it is in equilibrium.

Objects can be turned by their own weight. Some objects naturally return to a position of equilibrium if they are moved. Others fall over or roll to a new position.

The operator is turning this valve with two equal but opposite forces.

Here the object is unstable. When it is tilted it keeps falling.

A ball stays in a new position after it is tilted over.

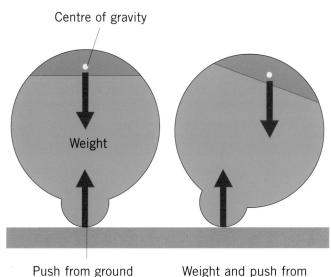

Centre of gravity

Weight

Push from ground

Weight and push from ground turn object further over

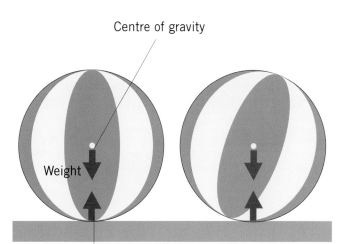

Centre of gravity

Weight

Push from ground

Centre of gravity still in line with the push from the ground

Repeating Movement

A playground swing is an example of a pendulum. It is made up of a weight in the end of a rope or chain. When you push a swing and let go, the swing keeps swinging backwards and forwards. The same movement is repeated again and again. Repeated motion like this is called **periodic motion**.

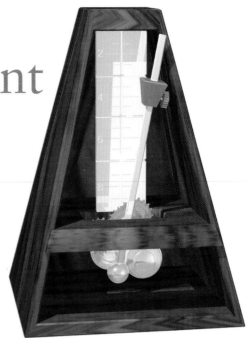

A metronome helps musicians play in time. The arm (acting as a pendulum) makes a click as it swings backwards and forwards.

CYCLES AND FREQUENCY

A complete movement of an object in periodic motion is called a cycle. A cycle of a pendulum is completed by a swing one way and a swing the other way. The number of cycles in one second is called the frequency of the motion. It is measured in hertz (Hz).

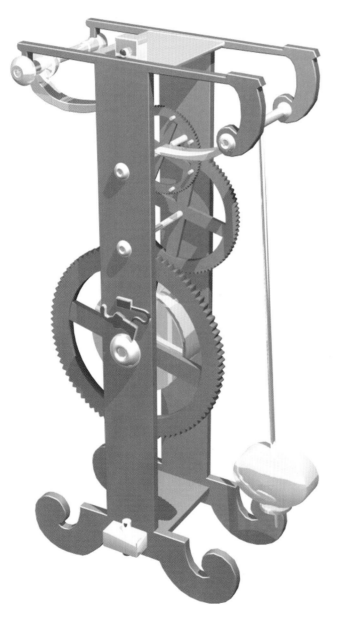

The regular swing of a pendulum keeps this clock going at a steady speed.

 **FACT FILE**

ANIMAL SOUNDS

• A bat produces sounds with **frequencies** up to 90,000 hertz. That's 90,000 cycles every second.

• Humans can hear sounds with frequencies up to 20,000 hertz. Dogs can hear sounds with frequencies up to 35,000 hertz.

INCREASING VIBRATIONS

The movements in periodic motion are often called vibrations. The size of a vibration is called its **amplitude**. Normally the amplitude of the vibrations gradually reduces. For example, the swings of a playground swing gradually die down until the swing stops. This happens because of friction and air resistance. Sometimes vibrations increase in amplitude. For example, if you push a swing each time it starts its downswing, it swings further and further. This is because you are pushing in time with the swing each time. The effect is called **resonance**.

WAVES AS VIBRATIONS

Waves such as waves in water and sound waves are made up of vibrations in periodic motion. For example, when a wave moves across the surface of a pond, the surface of the water moves up and down with periodic motion. Sound waves are made up of vibrations of the particles in the air.

A nuclear magnetic resonance scanner uses resonance to show the inside of a patient's body.

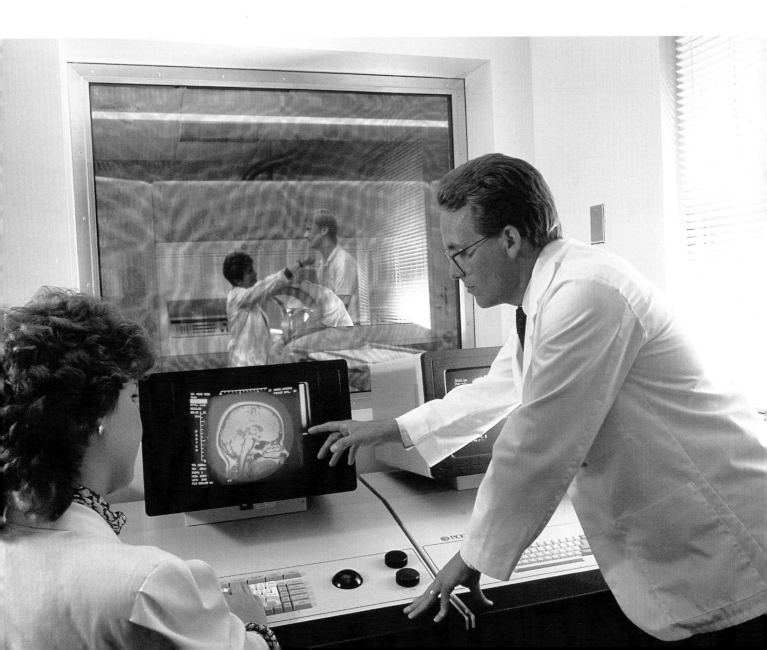

Circular Motion

Orbiting spacecraft and astronauts are in circular motion around the Earth.

Imagine you are sitting on a playground roundabout that is spinning round. You are moving in a circle, and every few seconds you complete one circle. Moving in a circle is called **circular motion**, and it is an example of periodic motion (see pages 32-33).

If an object moving in a circle does not speed up or slow down, it is travelling at constant speed. But because it is moving in a circle, it is always changing direction. That means its velocity is changing all the time (velocity is made up of speed and direction). So it must be accelerating all the time (acceleration is a change in velocity).

FORCES FOR CIRCULAR MOTION

Newton's second law of motion says that an object accelerates when a force acts on it. So there must be a force acting on an object that is in circular motion. This force is called **centripetal force**. It always acts towards the centre of the circle. Without it, an object would not move in a circle.

FEELING THE FORCE

To swing a ball on a string around your head, you have to keep pulling inwards on the string. Your pull is the centripetal force that keeps the ball moving in a circle. If the string broke, the centripetal force acting on the ball would disappear. The ball would carry on moving in the direction it was going when the string broke, and at the same speed. This is what happens when a discus thrower releases the discus after spinning round.

If you are in a fairground ride that moves you in a circle, you feel as though you are being pushed outwards, away from the centre of the circle. But you are not really. The seat is actually pushing you towards the centre of the circle.

Riders feel their seats pushing them inwards as they loop the loop.

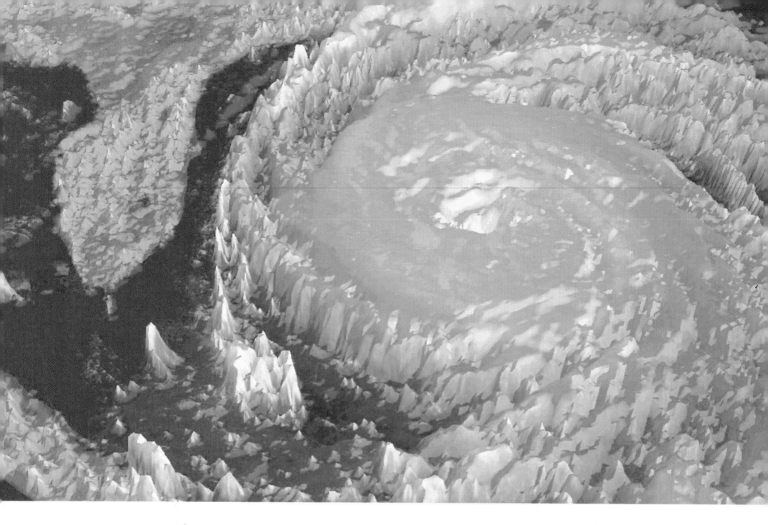

Angular Momentum

As air spirals into the centre of a hurricane it speeds up so that its angular momentum stays the same.

On page 23 we saw that objects have inertia, which is their tendency to stay still or keep moving in a straight line. In a similar way, objects have inertia when we try to make them spin round, and when we try to stop them spinning round. This inertia depends on the mass of the object. It also depends on the shape. For example, a ring has more inertia than a ball with the same mass because its mass is spread further from its centre.

Objects also have angular momentum because they are spinning. It depends on their inertia and how fast they are spinning.

An ice skater spins faster when she draws her arms inwards.

TEST FILE

MAKE A WHIRLPOOL

Fill a clear plastic drinks bottle with water. Add a few pieces of coloured paper to the water. Hold the bottle upside down over a sink (remove the top) and swirl it round to make the water spin. The water and paper will spin faster as it flows through the narrow neck so that momentum is conserved.

CONSERVING ANGULAR MOMENTUM

An object's angular momentum always stays the same. This law is called the conservation of angular momentum. If a spinning object changes shape, or moves nearer to the point it is moving round, its speed changes to conserve momentum. For example, if a spinning ice skater pulls her arms into her sides, some of her mass moves inwards. She spins faster so that momentum is conserved.

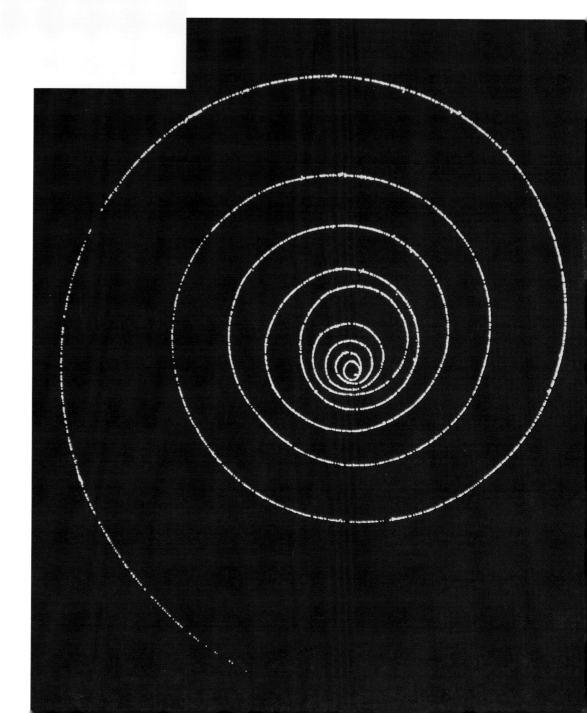

An electron follows a curved path as it moves through a magnetic field. It slows down and loses momentum because it loses energy, so it spirals inwards.

Pressure

Pressure is the force that pushes on a certain area. The greater the force acting on an area, the higher the pressure. The larger the area a force acts over, the lower the pressure. If you stand on one leg instead of two, the pressure you exert on the ground under your foot doubles, even though your weight stays the same. Pressure is measured in pascals. One pascal is equal to a force of one newton acting over an area of one square metre.

Water pressure in a pipe makes the water fly upwards to make a fountain.

PRESSURE IN LIQUIDS AND GASES

Liquids and gases always exert pressure on objects in them. In a liquid, pressure increases with depth. This is because of the water pushing down from above. At 10,000 metres down in the ocean, the pressure on an object is the same as an elephant standing on a postage stamp!

PRESSURE AND FLOATING

An object immersed in a liquid or a gas is always pushed upwards by the pressure on it. This push is called **upthrust**. If the upthrust is less than the object's weight, the object sinks. If it is greater than the object's weight, the object rises to the surface and floats. You can feel upthrust pushing upwards if you push an air-filled ball under the water.

Lift

Wing

Air flows faster over
top surface of wing

Air flows more
slowly over bottom
surface of wing

**An aircraft's wing produces an upwards force
called lift as air flows around it.**

PRESSURE IN FLOWING AIR

When air is flowing along, its pressure is
lower than when it is still. The faster it
flows, the lower its pressure becomes. This
effect is used by aircraft wings. When the
aircraft is moving forwards, air flows over
and under the wings. The shape of the wing
makes the air flow faster over the top than
underneath. So the pressure above the wing
is lower than under it. The higher pressure
under the wing produces a force called lift
that keeps the aircraft in the air.

**An aircraft must speed up on a runway until
its wings begin to work.**

FACT FILE

ARCHIMEDES

The Greek scientist Archimedes (see page 29)
discovered that upthrust is always equal to the
weight of water that the object pushes aside. It is
said that Archimedes realised the fact while he
was bathing, and shouted 'Eureka!', which means
'I have found it!'

Einstein and Relativity

At the beginning of the twentieth century, the German scientist Albert Einstein began to think about motion at extremely high speeds. For example, he wondered how he would look in a mirror if he was travelling along at the speed of light. Would the light reach the mirror, and would his image disappear? Einstein concluded that Newton's laws of motion would not work at very high speeds, and that it is impossible for anything to travel as fast as light.

THE SPECIAL THEORY OF RELATIVITY

Einstein wrote down his ideas in his special theory of relativity. The equations in the theory showed that if an object travels at speeds near the speed of light, strange things appear to happen. Distance shrinks, time slows down, and mass increases. But if you were travelling along with the object, everything would be normal. The special theory also showed that matter can be changed into energy. This discovery led to the invention of nuclear power stations and nuclear weapons.

Albert Einstein, who once said: 'Reality is just an illusion.'

HISTORY FILE

ALBERT EINSTEIN (1879-1955)

Albert Einstein was born in Ulm, in Germany. Einstein's teachers thought he was lazy and not very bright, but today he is thought of as one of the greatest scientists of all time. His special theory of relativity was published in 1905 and astounded the scientific world. Einstein won the Nobel Prize for Physics in 1921. From 1933 he lived in the USA.

If a car whizzed by a stationary observer near the speed of light it would look shorter.

But to the driver, the houses would look shorter!

PROVING THE THEORY

The speed of light is 300,000 kilometres per second. In normal life, things only travel at a tiny fraction of this speed, and the effects that Einstein predicted are too small to see. But very accurate clocks, called atomic clocks, flown round the world in spacecraft and high-speed aircraft, have shown that Einstein was right.

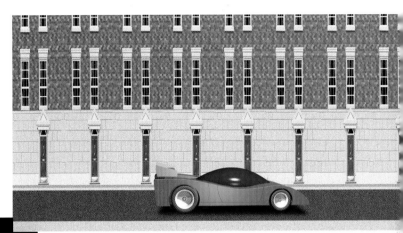

 **FACT FILE**

INCREASING MASS

Einstein's theory of relativity shows that an object's mass increases when it moves. But it must travel at 90 per cent of the speed of light before its mass is doubled.

In a particle accelerator, particles are accelerated to nearly the speed of light.

Space and Time

Albert Einstein also realised that space works a bit like a rubber sheet. If a heavy ball is placed on the sheet, it makes a dip in the sheet. If smaller objects are placed on the rubber sheet they roll towards the ball. This is what happens in space when gravity pulls objects towards each other. Space is not really like a rubber sheet, but this model shows Einstein's complicated idea of how the huge mass of stars and planets bend and squeeze space and time.

Einstein also predicted that light rays would be bent by the gravity of stars and planets, even though light rays have no mass. This theory was proved in 1919 when light rays from distant stars were seen to bend as they passed very close to the Sun.

FACT FILE

SQUEEZING THE EARTH

Black holes contain an incredible amount of matter in a very tiny space. For example, if the matter in the Earth was squeezed into a space to make it a black hole, it would be just 18 millimetres across!

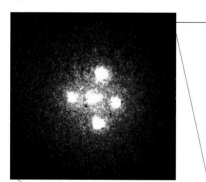

Light beams from star bent by gravity

Galaxy

Distant star

Photographs taken by the Hubble Space Telescope show that light is bent by the gravity of distant galaxies.

Images of star

Hubble Space Telescope

Light beams from distant stars are bent by the gravity of closer large galaxies. This means we see lots of images of a distant star.

An artist's impression of gas spiralling into a black hole.

The centre of the galaxy called M51. Astronomers believe that there is a giant black hole here.

 **FUTURE FILE**

WORMHOLES

Einstein's theory shows that there may be tunnels through space and time, which are called wormholes. Some scientists think that in the future we may be able to travel through them to get to other parts of the universe.

BLACK HOLES

A black hole is a place in space where the gravity is so strong that not even light can escape from it. A black hole forms when a star dies and collapses under its own gravity into a tiny space just a few kilometres across. In Einstein's rubber sheet model, a black hole would be like a bottomless hole. Nothing could climb out of the hole after it had fallen in.

Glossary

Acceleration A change in speed or velocity.

Air pressure The press that the air in the atmosphere makes on all the objects in it.

Air resistance The force made by the air that tries to slow down objects moving through the air.

Amplitude The size of a vibration of an object that is moving in periodic motion.

Atoms The tiny particles that all substances are made from.

Centripetal force The force acting towards the centre of a circle that keeps an object moving around the circle.

Circular motion The movement of an object in a circle.

Effort The force used to operate a simple machine such as a lever or pulley.

Electrons Tiny particles that are part of atoms and that have an electric charge.

Equilibrium When two or more forces cancel each other out.

Frequency The number of times something happens every second.

Friction A force that tries to stop two surfaces sliding past each other.

Fulcrum A point around which a lever or another object pivots.

Gravity The force that pulls every object towards the Earth.

Inertia The tendency of an object to stay still or keep moving.

Kinetic energy The energy an object has because of its movement.

Lever A simple machine made up of a bar fixed to a pivot.

Lift The upward force made by an aircraft's wings that keeps the aircraft up in the air.

Load The force that a simple machine such as a lever or pulley overcomes.

Magnetic field The area around a magnet where the magnet's force can be felt.

Mass A measure of the inertia of an object, or how much matter there is in an object.

Matter What everything in the universe is made from.

Moment The turning effect of a force.

Momentum An object's mass multiplied by its speed.

Nucleus The central part of an atom, made up of protons and neutrons.

Periodic motion Movement that is repeated again and again (for example, an object moving in a circle or swinging from side to side is in periodic motion).

Perpetual motion Motion that continues for ever without any push or pull to keep it going. It is theoretically impossible because of friction.

Potential energy The energy an object has because of where it is positioned.

Power The amount of energy used in a certain time.

Pressure The force pressing on a particular area.

Resonance When a vibration becomes larger and larger because the force acts in time with the movement.

Resultant force The overall force made by adding two or more forces together.

Simulation A mathematical model of a real-world event.

Terminal velocity The maximum velocity that a falling object reaches.

Turning effect The amount that a force makes an object turn.

Upthrust The upwards force made by water on an object in the water.

Vector quantity A quantity with both size and direction, such as force and velocity.

Velocity The speed and direction of an object.

Weight The force of gravity acting on an object.

Work The total amount of energy used to move an object from one place to another.

Further Information

PLACES TO VISIT

The Science Museum
Thousands of exhibits and hands-on activities on science and technology.
Science Museum, Exhibition Road, London, SW7 2DD
www.sciencemuseum.org.uk

Techniquest Science Discovery Centre
Over 100 hands-on exhibits and fascinating shows, plus a planetarium.
Techniquest Science Discovery Centre, Stuart Street, Cardiff, CF10 5BW
www.techniquest.org

BOOKS TO READ

Hands on Science: Forces and Motion by John Graham (Kingfisher, 2001)
Making Sense of Science: Forces and Movement by Peter Riley (Franklin Watts, 2004)
Science Files: Forces and Motion by Steve Parker (Heinemann, 2004)
Science the Facts: Forces and Motion by (Franklin Watts, 2004)
Straightforward Science: Forces and Movement by Peter Riley (Franklin Watts, 2003)

WEBSITES

www.bbc.co.uk/history/historic_figures
Learn about some famous scientists, including Newton and Archimedes

www.walter-fendt.de/ph11e/index.html
Features interactive experiments, including adding forces and pendulums

edheads.org/activities/simple-machines
Learn about simple machines in the home and garden

science.howstuffworks.com/relativity.htm
More about Einstein's theories of relativity

Index

Forces acting on a moving object

Burning rocket fuel creates a force that pushes the rocket upward.

Friction caused by moving through the air slows down the rocket.

The force of gravity pulls the rocket toward the Earth.